BOB COUSY

Rob Kirkpatrick

To Debbie

Published in 2002 by The Rosen Publishing Group, Inc.
29 East 21st Street, New York, NY 10010

Copyright © 2002 by The Rosen Publishing Group, Inc.

First Edition

All rights reserved. No part of this book may be reproduced in any form without permission in writing from the publisher, except by a reviewer.

Library of Congress Cataloging-in-Publication Data

Kirkpatrick, Rob.
Bob Cousy / by Rob Kirkpatrick.
p. cm. — (Basketball Hall of Famers)
Includes bibliographical references and index.
Summary: Profiles the life of Bob Cousy, a poverty-stricken New Yorker who went on to become an NBA All-Star for the Boston Celtics.
ISBN: 978-1-4358-8794-7
1. Cousy, Bob, 1928– —Juvenile literature. 2. Basketball players—United States—Biography—Juvenile literature. 3. Boston Celtics (Basketball team)—Juvenile literature. [1. Cousy, Bob, 1928– 2. Basketball players.] I. Title. II. Series.
GV884.C68 K57 2001
796.323'092—dc21

2001003212

Manufactured in the United States of America

contents

	Introduction	5
1.	From the Tenement to the Playground	9
2.	Making the Team	22
3.	College Crusader	33
4.	A Celtic Warrior	56
5.	Forging a Dynasty	68
6.	Life After the Celtics	90
	Glossary	104
	For More Information	107
	For Further Reading	109
	Index	110

introduction

One of the earliest photographs taken by Robert Joseph Cousy's parents foreshadowed his future. In it, Cousy is pictured as a toddler holding a ball similar to the type of ball that his entire life would one day revolve around. Many years later, when "Roby" had become a star basketball player, his mother would tell people that he had been holding a basketball in the photo. He hadn't been, but it made a good story. She said the picture proved that her son was destined to become a famous sports star.

It is easy to look back and say that Bob Cousy was born to play basketball, but his start in the sport was a rocky one. Although he eventually became one of the best basketball

For thirteen seasons with the Boston Celtics, Bob Cousy confounded NBA opponents with crafty moves that earned him the nickname "Houdini of the Hardwood."

Bob Cousy

players ever, Cousy spent most of his first year at Holy Cross College on the bench. Later he became a standout player for school. As a professional, he joined the National Basketball Association (NBA) to play for the Boston Celtics after tumbling around between draft pick decisions. Once there he helped them earn six NBA championships. In 1970, Cousy was inducted into the Naismith Memorial Basketball Hall of Fame.

Cousy was a huge success in basketball, but in reality, he was not a natural talent. He had to work extra hard to earn his place among America's sports heroes. For instance, although he did play basketball during his high school years, he twice unsuccessfully tried out for his high school basketball team. Here's another example of his determination to play the game he loved: When Cousy couldn't play basketball with his right hand after breaking that arm, he taught himself to temporarily maneuver the ball with his left hand. This same resolution would help him become one of the greatest players ever,

Introduction

earn him the NBA Most Valuable Player award in 1957, and allow him to make a name for himself as one of the most creative players that the sport of basketball has ever known.

From the Tenement to the Playground

Cousy was born on August 9, 1928, in New York City. His parents were French immigrants; his father, Joseph, was a farmer-turned–cab driver and his mother, Juliet, was a teacher who didn't learn English until the age of thirty.

Cousy spoke only French until he was five years old, when he began to learn English in school. Still, he would have a slight French accent throughout his life. Cousy also had a speech impediment. He had trouble making the sound for the letter *r*. When he tried to make this sound, it came out like the sound for the letter *l*. When he was young, children started to

Bob Cousy practices dribbling the ball during a Boston Celtics workout in 1953.

call him Frenchy, but when they noticed he could not pronounce the *r* sound, they changed the name to Flenchy.

The Cousy family lived on the East Side of New York in a small, tenement apartment with cracked windows and bricks, and without running water. They did not have much money, even though Cousy's father drove a taxi seven days a week to support his family. Joseph Cousy worked hard, but this was a tough time in America. The Great Depression had started in October 1929 after the stock market crash and, as a result, young Cousy knew only a life of poverty.

"I didn't feel very underprivileged. I had a whale of a good time out of life," he later wrote in his autobiography, *Basketball Is My Life*. He learned to play street games such as stickball, which mimicked the popular game of baseball, from the other kids on his block. Stickball has a pitcher, a batter, and bases to run, but instead of a bat, players use a broomstick.

From the Tenement to the Playground

Cousy and his friends passed the time with other activities, too. They went swimming in the East River and collected things like match covers and bottle caps. They also swiped, or stole, things such as fruit from street vendors. One day, Cousy and his friends decided to steal tire valve caps from several cars. Cousy got caught. It was a minor offense, and he didn't get in trouble, but it was the first of many times that his mischievous side would express itself.

Cousy and his friends had to create street games and other ways to pass the time because they did not have large open fields in which to play. Cousy's parents dreamed of living somewhere that had grass and playgrounds where he could run. Times were tough, but the Cousy family managed to save enough money to allow them to relocate to a nicer area, away from the inner city. They searched high and low for the perfect place in Brooklyn, Queens, and Westchester County before settling in St. Albans, a small section of Queens, Long Island. Cousy remembers, "Almost as soon as we drove into it, my mother clapped her hands and exclaimed, 'This—this is for us! I'm sure we'll find what we want here!'"

Back then, St. Albans was a mixture of apartment blocks and wide-open spaces. Cousy would have a cleaner place to live and space in which to play. He would also have other kids in the neighborhood to join him.

There was a big park in St. Albans called the O'Connell Playground, which housed a swimming pool, a handball court, and a baseball diamond. Cousy was watching kids play baseball on the diamond one day and thought the game looked fun. Midway through the game, the team in the field was missing a player when the shortstop had to go home. If the team wanted to keep playing, they would need a replacement. Cousy told them that he played shortstop. In truth, he had never played a real baseball game before. But because he was good at stickball, he figured he would be able to play this new game, too.

Andrew Jackson High School in St. Albans, Queens. Bob Cousy struggled to make his high school basketball team, but later became its star attraction by his junior year.

There was only one problem: Cousy didn't own a baseball glove. "Here, use mine," a boy on the other team said.

It was his first time playing a team sport. He discovered that he liked playing sports with a team of other boys. He also discovered that it helped to have big hands. He later remembered, "I wasn't very big, but I had huge hands and good eyes. I had learned how to swing a bat playing stickball, and I was a pretty good hitter. Even though I was one of the youngest kids in the gang, I held my own pretty well."

Cousy still liked the one-on-one sports that he played in school, such as handball, a game that is played by bouncing a ball off a wall. Because it is easy to get a game of handball together, Cousy frequently played the simple game all the time as a child.

A Lucky Break

When Cousy was thirteen, he fell from a tree and broke his right arm. Because he was right-handed, he mostly used his right arm when he

From the Tenement to the Playground

played sports. But now it seemed he would not be throwing any balls for a while.

One day soon after his accident, he saw one of his schoolmates by the handball court during recess. The boy asked Cousy to play.

"How can I play?" Cousy asked. "My right arm's in a cast."

"Use your left arm," the kid said.

Cousy agreed. The other boy was probably happy to have an opponent whom he could beat easily. Cousy was not used to using his left hand and must have looked funny trying. Cousy lost the game, but he had a lot of fun playing left-handed.

He could not have known it then, but the other boy's suggestion changed his life. Cousy kept playing handball with his left arm. He developed skills with his left arm that he normally wouldn't have developed. Later, when he began to play basketball, he could handle the ball well with both hands. He had become ambidextrous, a skill that would help him become a star.

From the Tenement to the Playground

A Whole New Ball Game

Baseball is often called America's pastime. In the first half of the twentieth century, it was the sport of choice for kids in America, and Cousy was no exception. Baseball was especially popular in and around New York City because of its three Major League teams: the New York Giants, the New York Yankees, and the Brooklyn Dodgers. Children in New York grew up debating which team was better, Cousy included. As a true Yankees fan, he enjoyed playing and talking about baseball with children in his new St. Albans neighborhood, especially about his favorite player, Joe DiMaggio, the team's famous center fielder.

In 1941, Cousy's favorite player set a Major League record by getting a hit in fifty-six straight games. But Cousy would soon forget all about his favorite sport in favor of another. That fall, Cousy started eighth grade. One day, he overheard some students

Baseball legend Joe DiMaggio of the New York Yankees

talking about the Andrew Jackson High School basketball team. It must have convinced him that basketball at Andrew Jackson High was important business! He told one of his friends that he should try practicing basketball during recess. The effect was amazing: The first time Cousy shot a basketball on the playground, it went into the hoop! Despite what his mother said about that baby picture, this was truly the first moment that Cousy had ever held a basketball. "Once I did," he later wrote, "I was hooked."

Meeting Morty

Even though Cousy liked basketball, the idea of playing on a team didn't occur to him until he was set to begin classes at Andrew Jackson High School, a new local hotbed for the sport. The coach, Lew Grummond, was considered one of the best in the area. Still, Cousy was only twelve years old and not so tall, and the older boys dominated the courts during recess.

From the Tenement to the Playground

One day a man came up to Cousy at O'Connell Playground and introduced himself as Morty Arkin. He was the new playground director. "I've been watching you," Arkin told him. "I think you could be pretty good."

Cousy didn't think too much about what Arkin had said. Soon, though, Arkin came up to him on the playground again. He liked how Cousy dribbled the ball. But he told him that he needed to learn how to shoot properly. He'd watched Cousy with the ball and explained to him that he was holding it incorrectly. Arkin demonstrated how to shoot the basketball more accurately—with your fingertips instead of your palms.

Arkin had also noticed how Cousy could dribble with both his right and his left hands. Cousy told him about the time he had broken his arm. Arkin told him the accident had been a good thing. It had taught him how to fully utilize his left hand. Arkin told him to keep practicing using both hands. He taught Cousy the advantages of being able to dribble and shoot from either side: Players on defense will try to stay between the ball carrier and the basket. A player that can only dribble and shoot from his right side will have a hard time going to the basket from the left. But if a player can dribble and shoot with his left hand, too, he can approach the basket from the left and still keep the ball away from defenders.

Cousy learned this and many other basic skills from Arkin. He also spent a great deal of time practicing basketball at the playground, going there before and after classes. He loved to play basketball, so he formed a makeshift team with other local young people. Eventually, they played other teams at the playground and joined a basketball league sponsored by the *Long Island Press*, a local newspaper. The more he played, the better he got.

But Cousy was thinking beyond O'Connell Playground. Whenever he played, he looked forward to joining the Andrew Jackson High

From the Tenement to the Playground

basketball team. He dreamed of becoming the best player that had ever played in the school. Soon, he thought, kids would be talking about him, like he often overheard them talking about the team during recess.

Making the Team

I had visions of taking Andrew Jackson High by storm," Cousy wrote in *Basketball Is My Life*. "I'd go out on that floor and kill them. Lew Grummond, the coach, would take one look at me and grab me for his varsity team. He would thank his lucky stars for me. I would be the greatest star in the school's history."

Cousy soon found out it wasn't that easy. About 250 kids showed up to try out for the team. Cousy, just fourteen years old, was only five feet, eight inches tall. He did not stand out in the group. He did well during the first practice, but not well enough to get Coach Grummond to notice him. On that fall day in 1942, Cousy did not make the team.

High school yearbook pictures of Bob Cousy

He cried when he found out he didn't make it, but he did not give up on basketball. He loved the sport and continued to be an active player on his *Long Island Press* League team. Cousy had so much fun playing, in fact, that he joined another team. It was formed from members of St. Pascal's youth organization, Cousy's Catholic Church, but that was still not enough for him. He also joined

Bob Cousy

the Laureltons, a team of Jewish children. Cousy now had three different teams on which to play the game he loved.

All of the practicing was beginning to make noticeable improvements in Cousy's game. Morty Arkin continued to work with Cousy on the playground, encouraging him to further develop the use of his left hand. Arkin also helped him develop a skill for which he would later be well known: the left-handed hook. Cousy worried less and less about the following year's varsity try-outs. This was the year he was certain to get Grummond's attention—or so he thought.

Try, Try Again

Cousy went out for the high school team in his sophomore year. Again, he failed. He was sad, but not as upset as he had been the first time it happened. He knew he could keep playing on community teams, such as his *Press* League team. He was happy while playing on the local courts, swimming on Jones Beach, and making friends in the neighborhood, but he still longed

Making the Team

for the opportunity to join his high school team. Cousy had a plan to help him satisfy his desire.

Although a player was not allowed on more than one *Press* League team, Cousy decided to join another group under a different division. In this way, he would not have to play against himself. He still needed to keep his identity a secret, though, so he borrowed a girlfriend's last name and signed up for the team as Bob "Kilduff." As Kilduff, he showed up for games wearing a red pom-pom underneath a winter hat. He thought this would make him look like he had long red hair. His disguise was laughable, but it showed how much he wanted to play.

Cousy continued getting advice from Arkin about the basics in basketball: how to sink the ball from all directions, and how to maneuver around the court. He kept practicing and playing. He still hoped he would get Grummond's attention.

One day he did. Cousy's *Press* League team played at the Andrew Jackson Community Center around the same time that Grummond became its director. During a scheduled game, Grummond watched Cousy's team play. The coach was impressed with how well Cousy could use his left hand. Coach Grummond even asked Cousy if he was left-handed. He said he liked players who could use both hands. He invited Cousy to the junior varsity (JV) practice the next day.

Once Grummond had noticed him, Cousy made the most of his chance. He showed up to JV practice and worked hard. Grummond finally put him on the team!

It was the first time that Cousy got to play on an organized, coached team. It was a good experience for him. Grummond taught the team set plays that helped them to score. In each play, each of the five members had separate responsibilities. They each had to know where to run, when to pass the ball, and to whom to pass it. Grummond assigned Cousy to a position as a point guard, a post normally held by shorter, faster players. Cousy was very quick and started offensive plays for his team.

Making the Team

Cousy and his teammates learned how to work together to make offensive plays most effective. Grummond was a strict coach who expected results. He made his team practice the same plays repeatedly. Grummond often had the JV team play against the varsity team. This helped the varsity team practice game situations. It also gave the JV good practice. They had to play very well to compete against the taller, bigger, and more experienced varsity team.

Playing against the varsity team was a challenge, but Cousy used that challenge to improve himself. Grummond saw that Cousy had talent. At the end of the year, he told him to keep practicing. If he did, Grummond promised he would make the varsity team in his junior year. This news thrilled Cousy. He had gone from hoping Grummond would notice him to possibly making the varsity team the following year.

On the Varsity

Cousy made the varsity team in his junior year. The Andrew Jackson basketball team played in the Queens Division of the Public School Athletic League, or PSAL. Cousy shone in his first game as a varsity player. He led the team in scoring with 28 points and helped them win the game.

This also made Cousy the talk of his hometown, St. Albans. The next morning, the *Long Island Press* ran a headline on the sports page that read: "Cousy Scores 28 Points." Cousy later recalled, "I was thrilled, and so were my folks. My mother carefully clipped the story and put it in a scrapbook. It was the first of many for her. Before I was out of high school, her book was full."

Indeed, Cousy was on his way to becoming a star player for Andrew Jackson High School. He helped the school win the Queens Division PSAL championship. Then, Andrew Jackson High made it to the city championships at Madison Square Garden. Known simply as the Garden, MSG is a famous sports arena. It is home to both the New York Knicks and the New York Rangers. Andrew Jackson High did well in the championship tournament, making it all the

Team photo of the Andrew Jackson High School Varsity Team in 1946. Bob Cousy is third from left in the front row.

way to the semifinal game before losing. Cousy did well in the tournament, too. He became well known by basketball fans in New York City, and his teammates elected him cocaptain of the Andrew Jackson High varsity team.

The Scoring Title

Cousy was a standout player after his junior year, yet he kept improving. He became the team's top scorer. In fact, he scored more than most people in the league. As the season progressed, two players battled for the PSAL scoring title: Cousy and Vic Hanson, a player from Long Island City High School. To fans and players alike, it was an exciting race. "Neither one of us picked up a long enough lead to stay in front from game to game," he remembered in *Basketball Is My Life*. "When he played and I didn't, he moved ahead. When I played and he did not, I moved ahead. We seesawed back and forth all season and attracted so much attention around Long Island that folks showed almost as much interest in our battle as they did in the league race."

Going into the last day of the season, Cousy and Hanson were tied. Both Jackson and Long Island City High had only one game left. Hanson's team played in the afternoon and scored 21 points. Cousy would need 22 points to win the title. He was averaging about 17 points a game, so scoring 22 would not be easy.

Making the Team

Andrew Jackson High played Far Rockaway High School in their last game. Cousy was nervous about the scoring race. Tensions were mounting as he scored only 8 points in the first half. He didn't think he had a chance anymore. During the second half, however, he relaxed and his attitude on the court loosened. Jackson was far ahead, and the other players started to pass the ball to Cousy as much as possible. Cousy kept scoring—20 points in the second half alone. This not only gave him 28 points for the game, but also the scoring title and status as the high school player to watch.

Cousy's skills carried him successfully into his senior year when he was named captain of the city's All-Scholastic Team. This team was made up of the best five high-school players in all of New York City. All of his determination was beginning to set him far apart from his peers.

But Cousy didn't focus only on the scoring race and his individual honors. He understood that basketball is a team sport. A player's

Bob Cousy

success is measured by his or her team's achievements. The Andrew Jackson team had another successful season in Cousy's senior year. With Cousy's help, they won the Queens Division title for the second straight year. The team did not do as well in the city championships, though. They were beaten in the quarterfinal game. Still, Cousy was positive that he was one of the best high-school players in all of New York.

Cousy began thinking about life after high school. He wanted to go to college and play basketball for a college team. He felt certain that he would get many scholarship offers. Cousy was on top of his game and on top of the world.

3

College Crusader

When a high school student is a very good athlete, colleges may try to recruit him or her. Because Cousy had had an excellent high-school basketball career, he was certain that many colleges would try to recruit him.

However, he was wrong. The only school that took an interest in Cousy and his basketball skills was Boston College. Boston College is a Catholic school, and Cousy and his family considered its offer. For a while, it even looked as if a match had been made.

Then, Cousy got a call from Ken Haggerty. Haggerty had been a star basketball player for Andrew Jackson High School, too. By then,

Haggerty was a junior at Holy Cross College, a Catholic school in Worcester, Massachusetts. Holy Cross had a young team with a new coach. Haggerty arranged for Cousy to meet with himself and with the coach, Alvin "Doggie" Julian. When they met, Cousy liked what he heard. Julian offered him a scholarship to go to Holy Cross.

Cousy now had two scholarship offers to play college basketball. He discussed his decision with his parents. They could tell he wanted to go to Holy Cross College, so they supported his decision. Cousy accepted the scholarship. Soon he would play for the Holy Cross Crusaders.

Once he was certain about his college career, Cousy was excited about his last summer at home. One afternoon, the coach of the Brooklyn College basketball team, Artie Musicant, invited some Andrew Jackson players to scrimmage against his team. High school players can have a tough time against college players, but the Jackson boys did fairly well.

College Crusader

They played several scrimmages against Brooklyn College. After one of the scrimmages, Musicant, also the athletic director of a summer camp, asked Cousy and Wes Field, another Andrew Jackson player, whether they had summer plans. Aside from playing basketball, neither did. Musicant encouraged Cousy and his teammate to join a basketball team at the camp while earning money for college.

Tamarack Lodge was a summer camp in upstate New York. It was located in the Catskill Mountains, in an area known as the Borscht Belt. There were many summer camps in the Borscht Belt in those days. Many families from the city went to these camps for summer vacations to explore the outdoors and get away from the city. Many people in these families were basketball fans and formed teams to compete against each other. The Brooklyn coach asked Cousy and his friend to play for the Tamarack Lodge team. They would also work as waiters or busboys, helping to earn money for college expenses. In exchange for their work,

Bob Cousy *(center left)* of Holy Cross College scrambles for a loose ball during an East-West all-star game at Madison Square Garden on April 1, 1950.

they would get free room and board, and possibly tips from lodge guests. Both Cousy and his friend agreed to spend the summer in upstate New York.

A Wrong Turn

Cousy was all set to head to the Catskills, but how would he get there? And how would he get around once he was there? Even though money was scarce, Cousy's father gave him $300 to buy a used car.

Cousy drove the car upstate to Tamarack. He also used it to go places when he and his friends got bored. One night, he and five other people packed into the car and headed to Ellenville, a nearby town. They never made it to the town. Cousy went speeding around a mountain road, headed fast into a sharp turn, and crashed the car through a guardrail. It turned over and headed over the mountainside. Cousy thought he and his friends were all going to be killed, but two trees stopped the car and kept it from rolling farther down the mountain.

College Crusader

The group in the car was very lucky. They suffered some cuts, but no one had any broken bones. Still, Cousy felt badly. He had ruined his car and had wasted his father's money. By the end of the summer, however, he had made some money from tips he had been given. He gave some of it to his parents to pay them back for the car, and put the rest of it in the bank for college.

Lost in the Crowd Again

When Cousy arrived in Massachusetts, he found an atmosphere that was much different than the one in St. Albans. He was hesitant at first, traveling through the industrial town of Worcester, but there were plenty of trees and long, rolling hills on the Holy Cross campus. He liked the college lifestyle, but he felt lonely surrounded by strangers. Once he began playing basketball, though, he fit in just fine.

In many ways, Coach Julian and Holy Cross had put college basketball on the map in New England. By the time Cousy walked onto the

Bob Cousy

court in 1946, East Coast college basketball teams were becoming more popular. Fans were familiar with college greats who had preceded Cousy, including Joe Mullaney, Dermie O'Connell, Charlie Bollinger, and Ken Haggerty.

Cousy immediately figured he would be a star on the Holy Cross team, just as he had been at Andrew Jackson High. He soon found that star status would not come easily. Coach Julian used a platoon system. This meant he used two teams of five players each in games. Each team took turns with the other. The first team started games and played more than the second team.

There were eleven players in all on the team. Julian said that his first team would be the five players who were returning from the previous year. This left six players to compete for five spots on the second team. Not only did Cousy not make the first team, he had to struggle to make the second. After so many years of constant basketball, Cousy was benched again.

 Bob Cousy makes a jump pass for Holy Cross College during an NCAA game in 1950.

Bob Cousy

Cousy made the second team, but he was angry. He resented that he had had to compete for a spot on the team. After all, he had a scholarship to play for Holy Cross. Why should he have to fight for a spot on the second team? He sulked and complained to friends, but never to his coach. The experience was an awkward beginning to his college career.

Still, the Holy Cross team did very well during Cousy's first year. The team played their games at the Boston Garden, a famous arena where the Boston Celtics played. Basketball fans came to the Garden by the thousands to watch the Holy Cross College basketball team. That year, they won twenty-seven games, losing only three. At one point, they won twenty-three straight games! In total, Cousy scored 227 points that first season, only a few short of their star, senior player George Kaftan. Holy Cross and Cousy went to the National Collegiate Athletic Association (NCAA) tournament and beat the U.S. Naval Academy, City College of New York (CCNY), and Northern Oklahoma College to win the championship.

College Crusader

Unhappy on the Inside

Most people would have thought that Cousy was happy being a part of one of the most well-regarded college teams in the country. But he thought that he was not getting adequate time on the court. Sometimes he played half a game or sometimes a third of a game—not bad for a first-year player on a championship team. But Cousy thought he deserved more playing time.

He was angry with coach Julian, and he regretted attending Holy Cross. After the NCAA tournament, Cousy returned to school and wrote a letter to Joe Lapchick, the basketball coach at St. John's University in New York. Cousy wrote that he wanted to transfer there instead.

Cousy didn't get the answer he expected. Lapchick wrote Cousy and said that he should stay at Holy Cross College, not only because Julian was one of the best coaches in the nation, but because he could get a quality education there. He felt it would be a mistake for Cousy to leave Holy Cross College just because he was frustrated after his first season.

Cousy was upset at first. The more he thought about Lapchick's advice, though, the more he realized that it was sound. He remembered his high school experience in basketball and how things had not always come easy for him. He decided to stay at Holy Cross. He told himself that he would be a model team member the following season.

"Doggie" Fights

Despite his determination to improve, things did not go smoothly during Cousy's second season. Cousy was a sophomore and he and Julian still did not get along well. Cousy believed that Julian was against him, even though he gained more playing time. Julian, meanwhile, did not like Cousy's demeanor. They put up with each other, but they disliked each other's attitudes.

The tension between the two boiled when Cousy missed a practice. Cousy and two friends

College Crusader

had been invited to a Saturday dance at a girls' school two hours away from Worcester. The Holy Cross team was scheduled to play a big game on Tuesday, so Julian had arranged a special practice for Sunday afternoon. Cousy had planned to go to the dance on Saturday and return to campus on Sunday in time for the special session.

It was a snowy weekend. On the way back to campus on Sunday, Cousy and his friends got into a minor accident with another car due to the icy road conditions. In the time it took to exchange license and registration information and temporarily mend the vehicles, Cousy was delayed. When he finally got back on the road, he drove slowly to avoid any other problems, but, by then, he had missed the practice altogether.

Julian was livid. He believed that Cousy had played in an outside game on Sunday. Cousy tried to explain what happened, but Julian did not believe him. He decided to punish Cousy by not allowing him to take his position in Tuesday's game.

Bob Cousy

Cousy sat on the bench and watched as the Holy Cross team was losing to its opponent, Loyola. The fans noticed Cousy was not playing, and they began chanting, "We want Cousy!" Finally, during the second half of the game, Julian backed down and put Cousy on the court with just five minutes left. In those five minutes alone, Cousy was able to score twelve points and win the game for Holy Cross.

After the game Cousy was very emotional. He was angry with Julian but relieved that he had gotten to play and to help the team win. Some players would have celebrated by showing up the coach, but Cousy didn't. He went instead into the locker room and cried. He had mixed feelings about his struggle to be a team player and his unhappiness with Julian's style of coaching. He was playing a game that he loved, but he was very unhappy.

For the rest of the season, Cousy and Julian said little to each other. They did not like each other, but they worked together for the good of the team. Julian always put Cousy

Holy Cross forward Bob Cousy flips the ball into the basket.

in the starting lineup, and Cousy always played hard.

Holy Cross College headed back to the NCAA tournament as defending champions. In the first game, Cousy scored 23 points as the Crusaders beat Michigan. But in the second round, he made only one of fourteen shots, and Holy Cross lost. Cousy was devastated. "It took me years to live down that game," he later wrote. It was a disappointing end to a difficult season for the sophomore player.

A New Season, A New Coach

Shortly after the NCAA tournament, Julian pulled Cousy away to explain that he had been hired to coach the Boston Celtics. Together they agreed that they had had a personality clash, despite their efforts to make their relationship work. They shook hands and parted friends. Years later, after Cousy went on to become one of New England's finest players ever, former coach Julian sent him a telegram expressing his admiration and

College Crusader

respect. Cousy still claims the telegram remains one of his most prized possessions.

In need of a new coach, the college hired Lester "Buster" Sheary. Cousy was delighted that the team would have a new outlook. Cousy loved playing for Sheary. He liked him as a person, and wanted to win games for him and for the rest of the team.

Cousy and his teammates had fun in practices. Even under Julian, the Holy Cross players practiced trick plays. They would fool around and make passes behind their backs, over their shoulders, and without looking. Cousy enjoyed these trick plays. He had used them in high school, too, but never during actual games. He resorted only to unusual game play if defenders were blocking him from making routine passes. Later, these unusual passes would earn Cousy a nickname that he still holds today: Houdini of the Hardwood. (The name Houdini came from Harry Houdini, the famous escape artist. Hardwood is a name for the surface of a basketball court.)

Holy Cross all-star Bob Cousy *(front row, far left)* poses with the members of the 1950 team of eastern college all-stars.

During his junior year at Holy Cross College, Cousy developed a trick play that later became one of his signature moves. He used it first in a game against Loyola at the Boston Garden. The game was tied with less than ten seconds left, and Cousy had the ball. He was on the left side of the court, dribbling toward the right, when a Loyola defender blocked his way. Cousy wanted to shift the ball to his left hand, but the defender gave him no

College Crusader

room to do so. Time was running out, so Cousy decided to use a trick move. He bounced the ball behind his back and took it with his left hand. The defender was so surprised that Cousy was able to go right past him. He shot a layup for the winning basket, and the crowd went crazy! They had never seen anything like it, although Cousy was not the only player that had used the move before: Bob Davies, a Seton Hall University player, had made a similar move in 1941. He later recalled, "I had never thought of such a maneuver. It just came to me the moment the situation forced me into it. It was one of those cases when necessity is the mother of invention. I was amazed at what I had done." Later, Cousy became famous for his style of playing.

Cousy would often be referred to as the ultimate point guard. His signature moves—behind-the-back feeds, half-court rocket shots, spinning dishes, and no-lookers—were the first of their kind seen on any basketball court in America.

Bob Cousy

Capping a College Career

Holy Cross College didn't win the NCAA championship under Coach Sheary, but they played well. In Cousy's senior year, Holy Cross College won twenty-six games in a row before losing to Columbia University. Cousy also had an excellent year. He was named to the all-American team, an honor given to the best five college players in the nation.

Cousy was established as one of the best college athletes in the United States, becoming a three-time all-American player. He won twenty-six straight games during his last season with Holy Cross College and helped the team finish second in the National Invitation Tournament (NIT).

He planned to play professionally in the National Basketball Association (NBA). He wanted to play for the Boston Celtics. Cousy liked Worcester, the small college town forty miles outside of Boston, and he wanted to live there. He had also enjoyed playing in the Boston Garden, where the Celtics played, as he had become a big fan of the team. And, although

College Crusader

Doggie Julian was now the Celtics' coach, Cousy wasn't worried. The two had met and had settled their differences just after Julian accepted the Celtics job. Cousy dreamed of playing for his longtime favorite team.

The Player Takes a Wife

The summer after Cousy graduated from Holy Cross College, he moved into a cabin in Worcester with several friends. He still dreamed of life as a professional basketball player. The future looked bright for Cousy, but something was missing.

In his senior year of high school, Cousy had begun dating Marie "Missy" Ritterbusch. She had gone to a parochial, or religious, school for girls in Brooklyn, and the two had dated for a few years but they had a fight during their junior years and had separated. Even though they drifted apart during Cousy's senior year, he never forgot her. He wrote to her after graduation, and she wrote back. He found out that she was living in Winchendon, a town about

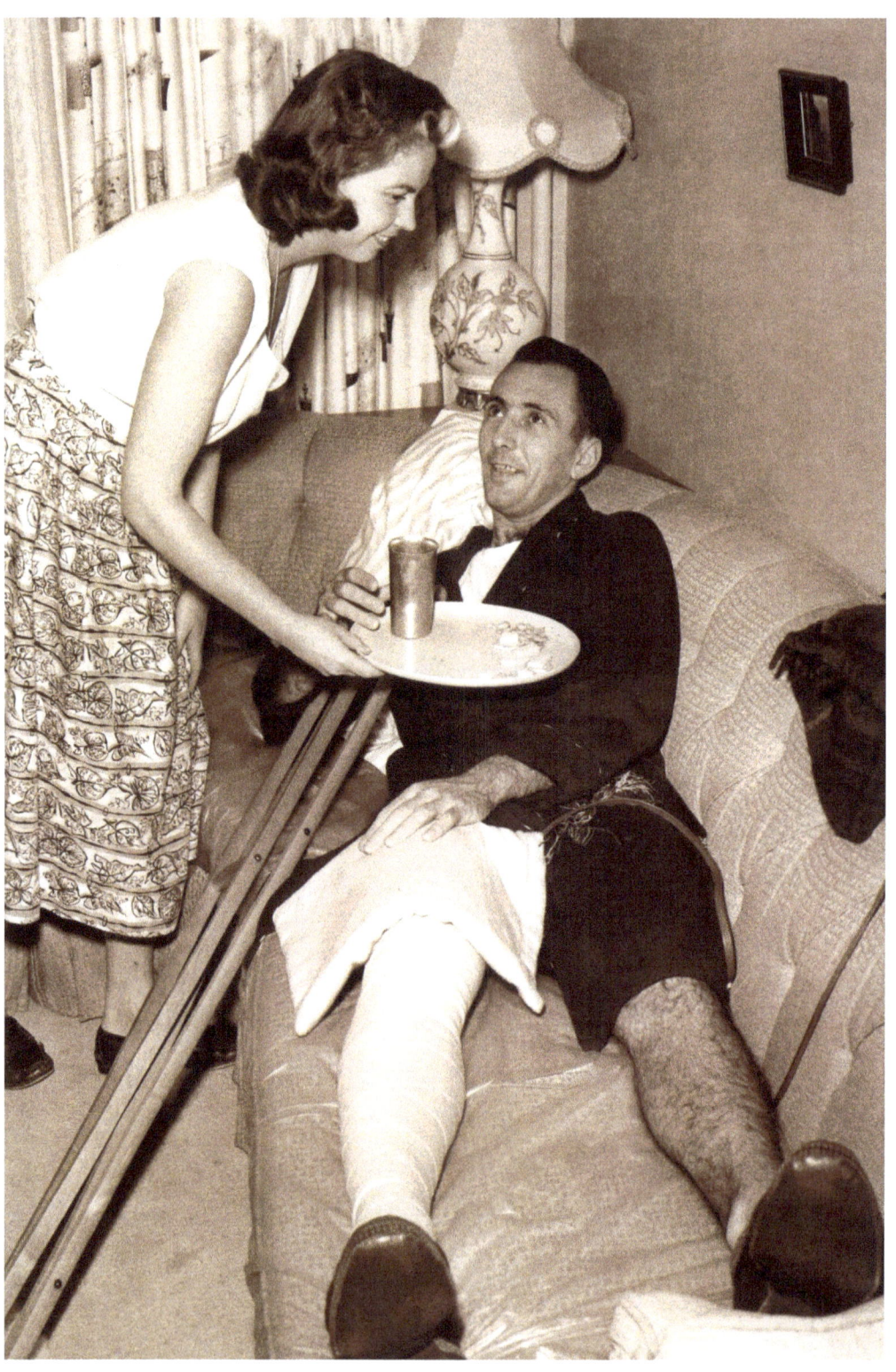

College Crusader

an hour away from Worcester. She invited him to come to see her. They quickly started dating again. This time, Cousy was determined not to lose her. He proposed, and she accepted.

By the fall, Cousy was living in an apartment that was owned by Al and Helen Kalil, a Syrian couple. The Kalils arranged for Cousy and Ritterbusch to hold their marriage ceremony at the Syrian-American Club in Worcester. The two were married on December 9, 1950.

Cousy now had a wife. By the time he got married, he also had a new job: professional basketball player for the Boston Celtics!

Marie Cousy at home with her injured husband in November 1957

A Celtic Warrior

Today, the media gives much attention to NBA draft picks. For weeks before the draft, fans and columnists alike wonder which teams will pick which players. The NBA draft is televised every year. Teams take turns announcing the players they have selected. When a team's turn comes, a representative from that team gives the name of a player to the league commissioner, who stands at a podium and announces the selection. Generally, it's a huge spectacle.

In 1950, the NBA was different from what it is today. The draft was not a very big deal. It was so casual, in fact, that Cousy's name was drawn out of a hat!

A Celtic Warrior

The story of how Cousy became a Celtic is a long one. It is also the beginning of another: the story of one of the most successful careers in NBA history.

At first, Cousy was not even going to play for the Celtics at all. They did not draft him. Back then, NBA teams often drafted players from colleges in their own area. This way, they got players who were popular with local fans. Walter Brown, the owner of the Celtics, wanted Cousy to play for them. But Cousy played the guard position. What the Celtics needed was a center. They drafted Chuck Share, an all-American center from Bowling Green University. The Tri-Cities Blackhawks drafted Cousy. The team played in an area that was between three small cities: Moline and Rock Island in Illinois, and Davenport in Iowa.

Cousy was very disappointed. He did not even know where the "Tri-Cities" were. He made a trip to Boston to talk with Walter Brown. Cousy begged Brown to get him on the

A Celtic Warrior

Celtics, but Brown said there was nothing he could do. The Blackhawks got the rights to Cousy when they drafted him.

By that time, Cousy's old coach, Doggie Julian, had taken a job coaching Dartmouth College. The Celtics had a new coach named Arnold "Red" Auerbach. The local newspapers criticized Auerbach for failing to select Cousy in the draft, because he was a local favorite. When a reporter asked Auerbach at a press conference why he didn't draft Cousy, Auerbach was quoted as saying, "Am I supposed to win or worry about the local yokels?" Another reason why Cousy wasn't drafted was because he wasn't as tall as the other players. For the time being, Cousy gave up on his dream of playing for the Celtics. He decided to meet with the owner of the Tri-Cities Blackhawks. Cousy and the Blackhawks owner, Ben Kerner, met at Kerner's office in Buffalo, New York, to talk about a contract.

Legendary Boston Celtic coach Red Auerbach led his team to nine NBA championships in sixteen years. Because of this record, he is often referred to as the architect of the greatest dynasty in NBA history.

Bob Cousy

Let the Negotiations Begin

When an NBA team drafts a player, it does not necessarily mean that he will play for that team. It means the team has "rights" to the player. That team is the only one in the league that may offer contract terms to the player. Usually, that player also has an agent to help him gain the best contract terms possible. The agent and the player talk about the contract offer until both are completely satisfied with its terms. If they like the offer, the player signs the contract and becomes an employee of the NBA team. If either the agent or the player does not like the offer, negotiations may continue.

Cousy, like many players in 1950, did not have an agent. He met with Kerner personally. Kerner offered Cousy $6,500 to play for his rookie (first) season, but Cousy wanted $10,000. It did not look as though they would agree on a contract, so Cousy flew home. Later that week, Kerner convinced Cousy to come back to Buffalo to continue negotiations. Eventually, the two agreed on an amount of

A Celtic Warrior

$9,000 and Cousy signed. He was now a professional basketball player!

The Tri-Cities Blackhawks had drafted and signed Cousy, but for some reason, they decided to trade him. They traded him to the Chicago Stags, another NBA team. Before the season began, the Stags folded. Meanwhile, Cousy thought he was still on the Blackhawks team. In reality he was a player *without* a team.

The NBA decided to take the ex-Stag players and divide them among the remaining NBA teams. However, the New York Knicks, Philadelphia 76ers, and Boston Celtics argued over three players: Cousy, Max Zaslofsky, and Andy Philip, all promising young athletes with impressive scoring records. Cousy was a good player. Zaslofsky and Philip were proven athletes who'd both made the NBA all-star team. The president of the NBA called a meeting in New York to decide which team would get which player. The teams agreed to pick the names of the three players from a hat to make the decision. The Knicks chose first and nabbed

Bob Cousy

Zaslofsky's name. The '76ers picked Philip's name. Finally, the Celtics drew Cousy's name. "When I drew Cousy," Walter Brown later said, "I could have fallen on the floor."

Cousy did not know any of this was going on, but he knew something was in the works. The Blackhawks' owner had told Cousy not to report to Tri-Cities yet. Why didn't Kerner want him to join the team for practices, Cousy wondered. Something must be up, he figured.

He was right. Soon after the meeting in New York, the Celtics' Walter Brown called Cousy. He told him to get in his car and to drive to Boston. Cousy's dream had come true. He was now a member of the Boston Celtics!

Rookie Sensation

Cousy had always felt that he was a special basketball player. He also knew things had not always come to him easily. He had twice failed to make his high-school junior varsity team. He had had to battle for playing time in his first year on his college team. Now, he was among

Cousy demonstrates his behind-the-back pass in this profile photo.

Bob Cousy

professional players for the first time, and no one knew how well he would play.

Any doubts that people had about Cousy quickly went away. The twenty-two-year-old fit right in during his rookie year with the famous Boston team. All of his years of practice on the playground, in high school, and in college had helped him develop excellent skills. Celtics fans were surprised by how well Cousy could dribble, pass, and shoot the ball.

During that first season (1950–1951), Cousy averaged almost 16 points per game. He also helped his teammates score points, too. When a player makes a pass to a player who scores a basket, the first player is credited with an assist. Cousy averaged just under 5 assists per game that first year. Back then, every basket was worth 2 points. (There was no 3-point basket yet.) By averaging almost 5 assists per game, Cousy helped other teammates score an average of 10 points per contest. Add these points together and it's easy to see that the rookie accounted for

Bob Cousy (number 14) and Al McGuire of the New York Knicks scramble for a loose ball during an NBA playoff game on March 16, 1954.

almost 26 points per game. That's not bad for a "local yokel."

The added offense that Cousy brought to the Celtics helped the team win more games. Boston finished the 1950–1951 season with a record of 39–30. It was the first time that the Celtics had ever finished a season with a winning record. Cousy was playing well, and he was helping his team win.

A Record Night

On February 27, 1959, Bob Cousy set an NBA record by tallying 28 assists in a 173–139 victory over the Minnesota Lakers. Since then, only two players have had more assists in one game. Scott Skiles now holds the record with 30.

Not a Sophomore Jinx

Sometimes, a player may have a good rookie season but a tough second year. This can happen for many different reasons. Sometimes the other players learn how to play well against a particular player once they become more familiar with his style in the second year. Or he falls into a slump and simply loses confidence. And sometimes that rookie success is just luck. When a player has a promising first year but a disappointing second year, it's called the sophomore jinx.

Cousy, however, did not suffer from a sophomore jinx. He became even better in his second year. He averaged more than 21 points,

A Celtic Warrior

which was the third-highest average in the league. He had more than 6 assists per game, the second-highest average in the league. During Cousy's second professional season, the Celtics finished in second place in the Eastern Division with a record of 39–27. Boston had become a winning team, and Cousy was a big reason for its success.

Fans were not the only ones who appreciated Cousy's playing style. This spectacular sophomore earned the respect of sportswriters and fellow basketball players, too. After the 1951–1952 season, Cousy was named to the NBA First Team, that is, a list of players who are considered the best at their positions. This was a great honor for Cousy, and it was the first of many he would receive. He was named to the NBA First Team after each of the next nine seasons!

5

Forging a Dynasty

By the 1952–1953 season, Cousy had proven that he could play in the NBA. He also had proven that he could help the Celtics win games. During his first two seasons with the Celtics, the team made the playoffs. But both times, however, they lost to the New York Knicks in the first round. The Celtics were a good team, but they were not a great team—yet.

Part of building a winning team is adding good players. It's great to have a player like Cousy, but basketball is a team game. One player cannot win games by himself. The Celtics had another very good player in Ed McCauley. Then, the team got Bill Sharman before the 1951–1952

Forging a Dynasty

season. Sharman could shoot the ball well, and score many points. The more these players were together on the court, the better the team became. In the 1952–1953 season, Cousy, McCauley, and Sharman helped the Celtics score more points than any other team in the league. The Celtics set a team record with forty-six games, but finished in third place behind the New York Knicks and the Syracuse Nationals. The Knicks and the Nationals both won forty-seven games that year. Still, the Boston Celtics were on their way to becoming one of the top teams in the NBA.

Playoff Action

During the first round of the playoffs, the Celtics faced the Nationals in a best-two-out-of-three series. This means that the first team to win two games won the series. The Celtics won the first game. The second game went down in history as a classic moment in sports. At the end of regulation time, the Celtics and the Nationals were tied. To settle the score, the two teams

Forging a Dynasty

played an overtime period. The teams were tied after the first overtime period, too. Then they played a second overtime. Again, the period ended with the teams tied. The teams were still tied after a third overtime! Finally, after the fourth overtime, the Celtics came away with more points. They won the game 111–105. Cousy had a big part in the win. He scored 50 points that day!

The Celtics lost to the Knicks in the next round of the playoffs. But people would be talking about Cousy's performance against Syracuse for a long time. People within the league had known he was a very good player, but Cousy was becoming a legendary player.

The Celtics had become the top scoring team in the NBA. Cousy led the league with more than 7 assists per game in the 1953–1954 season, but again, Boston lost in the second round of the playoffs.

If the team could score so many points, why did they lose? They had trouble keeping other teams from scoring. The Celtics were not a

Cousy (number 14) battles Ernie Vandeweghe of the New York Knicks for a rebound during an NBA playoff game in 1953.

good defensive team. In the 1954–1955 season, the Celtics became the first team in NBA history to average 100 points per game. However, they gave up 101.5 points per game to the opposition. They finished with a record of 36–36 that season, and lost to Syracuse in the first round of the playoffs. They had a slightly better record the following season at 39–33. Again, though, they lost to Syracuse in the first round.

The Missing Piece

In 1956, Red Auerbach knew he had to do something. His team had done well during regular-season play, but they did not have much success. The Celtics needed somebody who could help them play better defensively. The Celtics got that person in a trade with the St. Louis Hawks. His name was Bill Russell.

Russell was a six-foot-ten-inch center who had played for the University of San Francisco. The Hawks picked Russell in the 1956 draft. Then, the Celtics traded Ed McCauley and another player to the Hawks for Russell.

Bill Russell as a member of the University of San Francisco basketball team in 1956. His addition to the Celtics was pivotal to the team's impressive championship record between 1957 and 1966.

As soon as Russell joined the Celtics, he made a big difference in the playing style of the team. He used his size and strength to stop the other team from scoring. He could block shots. He could also jump high to grab the ball after the other team missed a shot. This move is called a rebound. It's important for a team to get as many rebounds as possible. When a player gets a rebound, he or she stops the other team from trying to score. A rebound also gives his team a chance to score the next point.

The team also had a good player in 1956 Celtic draft pick rookie Tommy Heinsohn because he was good at both offensive and defensive play. He could also score rebounds. Many Celtics fans remember players such as Russell and Heinsohn who helped the Celtics become a complete team. Heinsohn, as well as other players, were beginning to notice Cousy's talents, too. The Celtics were now stopping their opponents from scoring, as well as scoring themselves.

Cousy was surrounded by a number of very good players that helped him shine. Celtics fans remember how Russell used to get a rebound and pass the ball quickly to Cousy who would dribble the ball toward the opposing team's basket. Then, he would shoot or pass the ball to an open teammate (one who was not being guarded by a defender). Many times, Cousy would set up an offensive play before the other team could get back and play defense.

Forging a Dynasty

This is called a fast break. Cousy led countless fast breaks for the Celtics. Tommy Heinsohn said, "What Russell was on defense, that's what Cousy was on offense—a magician. Once that ball reached his hands, the rest of us just took off, never bothering to look back. We didn't have to. He'd find us. When you got into a position to score, the ball would be there."

With players like Cousy and Russell, the Celtics became a great team in the 1956–1957 season. They finished the regular season with the best record in the NBA at 44–28. Cousy was a big reason for the team's success. In fact, he was given a great honor and was named the NBA's Most Valuable Player. He became the top player on the best team in the league.

A Winner at Last

When the Celtics could play both offense and defense well, they did much better in the NBA playoffs. They made it all the way to the 1957 NBA Finals and faced the St. Louis Hawks, the champions of the Western Division. The Finals

Forging a Dynasty

are a best-four-out-of-seven series. The first team to win four games is the NBA champion.

It was a very tough series and both teams played well. The first two games were at the Boston Garden with the Hawks and the Celtics splitting wins. The next two games were played in St. Louis. The teams split these games as well. The Celtics won Game 5 in Boston, but the Hawks came right back and won Game 6 in St. Louis. Each team now had three wins.

Game 7 of the 1957 Finals was a fierce battle. The Celtics and Hawks were tied at the end of regulation time. They were still tied after the first overtime period. Finally, the Celtics emerged from the second overtime with a 125–123 win. The Celtics had won the series and were finally NBA champions!

When the game ended, Cousy jumped for joy. It hadn't been one of his better games, but he didn't care. "I hadn't contributed much to the particular game," he wrote in *Basketball Is My Life*, "but I had satisfied my lifelong ambition. I was with a winner at last."

Bob Cousy delivers a successful over-the-shoulder shot during a regular-season NBA game against the Minneapolis Lakers at Boston Garden on November 10, 1957.

The Celtics followed that win with another fine season in 1957–1958. Cousy led the league in assists, and the Celtics won the NBA's Eastern Division. They went back to the NBA Finals again against St. Louis in 1958. Unfortunately for Boston, Russell suffered an ankle injury in Game 3. He could not play in Games 4 or 5. After Game 5, the Hawks led the series by one win. Russell played in Game 6, but his injury did not allow him to play well. As a result, the Hawks won both the game and the series.

Building a Dynasty

Cousy, Russell, and the other Celtics players were disappointed that they did not win the NBA Finals in 1958. This only made the team more determined to win the following year. The Celtics also added young rookie players such as K.C. Jones and Sam Jones. The 1958–1959 Celtics team went 52–20. They would go on to beat Syracuse in the Eastern Conference finals in a tough, seven-game series.

Bob Cousy receives the Most Valuable Player award during a half-time ceremony at the NBA All-Star Game on January 21, 1958.

The Celtics went on to face the Minneapolis Lakers in the NBA Finals. The Minneapolis Lakers, who would later become the Los Angeles Lakers, had a young player named Elgin Baylor. But the Celtics had many great players. They swept the Lakers four games to zero and won their second NBA championship.

The Celtics had gone to the Finals three years in a row and had won two titles. Many teams

Bob Cousy gives four campers tips on handling a ball at Graylag, his basketball camp in Pittsfield, New Hampshire, in 1959.

would be satisfied with that success. Cousy and the Celtics were happy, but they wanted more. In fact, the Celtics were on their way to becoming one of the most successful teams in sports history.

During the 1959–1960 season, the Celtics faced the Philadelphia Warriors in the Eastern Conference finals. The Warriors had a rising star named Wilt Chamberlain, who was known as a high scorer. Chamberlain won the league's Most Valuable Player award that year. Again, the Celtics proved that a great team was even better than a great player, and they won the series four games to two. Then they defended their league championship by beating the Hawks in seven games.

The following season, the Celtics won fifty games. They lost only two games during the entire postseason. Boston beat St. Louis in the Finals four games to one. It was the Celtics' third championship in a row, and the fourth in six seasons.

In truth, they were just warming up. In the 1961–1962 season, they went back to the division

Forging a Dynasty

finals. Again, they faced Chamberlain and the Warriors. The Celtics and Warriors split the first six games, and the Celtics slipped by in Game 7, 109–107. Boston went to the Finals and faced the Lakers, who now played in Los Angeles. The Los Angeles Lakers won three of the first five games. It looked as though they were going to knock off the defending champions, the Celtics. But the Celtics won Game 6 in a score of 119–105 and won Game 7 in overtime, with a final score of 110–107. Again, the Celtics were champions! They had set an NBA record by winning four championships in a row. Boston was not just a great team, they were a dynasty.

The Last Hurrah

Bob Cousy had become a star player on one of the best teams in sports history. He had built an incredible sports career. However, he was aging. He was thirty-four years old. He had played in the NBA for twelve years. He knew he could not be a record-breaking player forever. Before the

Bob Cousy

1962–1963 season, Cousy announced that he would retire by season's end.

This time, though, things seemed different for the team and for Cousy. Just before the playoffs, *Sports Illustrated* wrote an article criticizing the team. "The Boston Celtics are an old team," the article read. "Tired blood courses through their varicose veins."

It was a challenging season for Cousy. The Celtics had a younger player, K.C. Jones, who also could play point guard. Cousy feared he was going to be replaced. Cousy said, "People don't know what they're talking about when they say the older you are the less you notice the tension. Each day you have to prove yourself all over again."

The Celtics went back to the Finals in 1963. It had become a yearly tradition for the Celtics. They faced the Los Angeles Lakers. Boston won the first two games and it looked like the series might be an easy win. Then, however, the Lakers won two of the next three games. People wondered whether the Celtics were getting tired.

 Bob Cousy breaks into tears while making a speech to over 15,000 fans prior to his last regular-season game at Boston Garden on March 17, 1963.

Bob Cousy

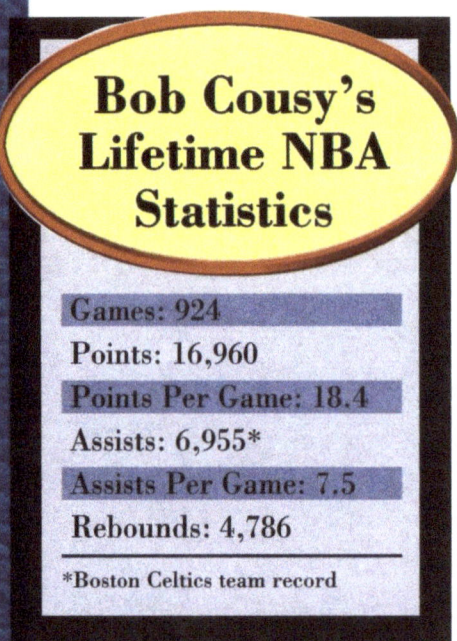

Bob Cousy's Lifetime NBA Statistics

Games: 924
Points: 16,960
Points Per Game: 18.4
Assists: 6,955*
Assists Per Game: 7.5
Rebounds: 4,786

*Boston Celtics team record

Would the Lakers end the Celtics dynasty?

Game 6 was played in the Lakers' home city, Los Angeles. Even though the Celtics gained a 9-point lead early in the fourth quarter, they suffered a bad blow. Cousy tripped and sprained his ankle. He had to come out of the game. With Cousy on the bench, the Lakers made a comeback. They pulled within one point of the Celtics late in the fourth quarter. Celtics coach Auerbach needed Cousy to play. Cousy came off the bench and played despite his sprained ankle. Miraculously, he helped the Celtics increase their lead. As time ran out on the clock, Cousy dribbled around the court and kept the ball away from the Lakers players. The final buzzer sounded, and the Celtics had won again with a final score of 112–109. Cousy threw the ball

Forging a Dynasty

into the air. It was their fifth championship game in a row! Cousy had proven that he was not too old to lead his team to an NBA title.

Boston "Tear" Party

Cousy ended the 1963 season by leading the Celtics to yet another NBA title. It was his last season as a Celtics player. He had been a great player, appreciated by the city of Boston and Celtics fans. At the beginning of the next season in October, the team and its fans held a special night to celebrate Cousy's career. Thousands of fans packed the Boston Garden. He was asked to give a speech to the crowd. Cousy became very emotional. When he became speechless, a fan

Career Highlights

NBA MVP
1957

All-NBA Team
First Team 1952–1961
Second Team 1962–1963

NBA All-Star Game MVP
1954 and 1957

NBA Championships
1957, 1959, and 1960–1963

The Boston Celtics pose with president John F. Kennedy while on a tour of the White House in 1963. Bob Cousy is second from left in the front row.

yelled, "We love ya, Cooz." He was so emotional that the fans began to cry. People later called it the Boston "Tear" Party.

How popular was Bob Cousy? President John F. Kennedy sent a telegram to Cousy for the celebration. It read: "The game bears an indelible stamp of your rare skills and competitive daring." Celtics owner Walter Brown also commented on Cousy's achievements: "The Celtics wouldn't be here without him. If he had

Forging a Dynasty

played in New York, he would have been as big as Babe Ruth. I think he is anyway." As a testament to Cousy's achievements with the now-famous Boston team, the Celtics decided to retire his number. This means that no other player may wear his number on a Celtics' uniform. Cousy's number, 14, will never appear on a Celtics uniform again. Cousy ended his professional career with six championships. He had played in thirteen all-star games, had led the NBA in assists eight times, and had won an NBA Most Valuable Player award. He had done more than he, or anyone, could have ever dreamed.

6

Life After the Celtics

When a great player retires, he may have a difficult time switching gears to a less public lifestyle. Cousy had spent most of his life playing in organized basketball. He had to find something else to do with his time.

From Player to Coach

Cousy had almost gone to Boston College after high school and, after his NBA career, Boston College wanted him again. This time they asked him to coach their men's basketball team. He knew the game well, and he was popular with basketball fans in Boston. Cousy agreed to become the next Boston College coach. It was a great fit.

Life After the Celtics

It can be hard for a great player to become a coach. A player such as Cousy may have a difficult time working with players who are not as talented as he had been. A player-turned-coach may become impatient with his team. However, Cousy did a fine job. In six years under Cousy, the team went 117–38. The team won at least twenty consecutive games four times. In one season, Boston College even went to the finals of the National Invitation Tournament (NIT).

Despite his success, Cousy grew tired of the college game. He did not enjoy having to recruit new players. A coach must often travel around the country and try to convince good players to play for his college. Cousy disliked all the traveling and was also looking for a new challenge. As a result, he resigned as Boston College's basketball coach after the 1968–1969 season.

Back in the Pros

An NBA team, the Cincinnati Royals, hired Cousy to coach them in the 1969–1970 season.

Coach Bob Cousy *(second from right)* leads members of his Boston College basketball team in a dribbling routine during a workout at Madison Square Garden on March 11, 1965.

This gave Cousy, who had been longing to rejoin the world of professional sports, a chance to be part of the professional game again. Unfortunately, the Royals were not a very good team and did not draw many fans. The Royals thought that having Cousy as coach would increase their fan base.

The Royals also knew fans would like to see the great Cousy play again. The team convinced Cousy to become a player-coach. (A player-coach plays for his team and coaches it at the same time.) This can be a very complicated job. It is hard enough to play a professional sport. It is more difficult to play while having to run the whole team, too. Fans were curious to see how the great Cousy would do as player-coach. Ticket sales went up 77 percent during that season.

Coaching Woes

When Cousy agreed to be a player-coach, he was forty-one years old. He became the oldest person to be active on an NBA roster. However, he had

Bob Cousy, basketball coach at Boston College, cries during a press conference in 1967, in which he denies willingly providing bookmakers with information for basketball point spreads.

not played professional basketball in more than six years. Cousy was not the athlete that he used to be. As a result, the experiment did not last long. He was active for only seven games that year.

Cousy had done a great job as a college coach, but he could not turn the Royals into winners. Fans stopped coming to games. The

Royals moved to Kansas City in 1972, where they became the Kansas City Kings. But things did not get much better for the team there. Cousy quit as coach early in the 1973–1974 season with the team having a career record of 141–209.

Back Where He Belonged

After Cousy left coaching, he needed to find a new career. The Boston Celtics and their fans still remembered what a great player Cousy had been for them. They also knew how well he understood the game. However, they didn't want Cousy back on the court; they wanted him to be a television broadcaster for Celtics games. It proved to be a perfect match. Cousy has worked as broadcaster for the Celtics ever since. Today, Celtics fans can tune in to hear expert commentary from a skilled Hall of Famer.

In 1996, the NBA turned fifty years old. Commissioner David Stern decided to honor the fifty greatest players from the league's first fifty years. He named a panel of basketball media, former players and coaches, current and former

Life After the Celtics

general managers, and team executives to select the players to be so honored. Cousy was voted to the list of the NBA's fifty greatest players, which included notable athletes such as Michael Jordan, Charles Barkley, John Stockton, and Patrick Ewing. It also included older players, such as Wilt Chamberlain, Pete Maravich, and former Celtic teammates Sam Jones, Bill Sharman, and Bill Russell.

In 1999, the ESPN cable network announced its list of the 100 best North American athletes of the twentieth century. The list included great stars of baseball, football, basketball, hockey, boxing, track and field, and even horseracing. There have been thousands of great athletes in all types of sports in the twentieth century, but people still remember Bob Cousy's talent. He was voted 94 in a listing of the 100 best athletes of the century.

Into the Hall

The Naismith Memorial Basketball Hall of Fame is located in Springfield, Massachusetts, and is

A concerned Bob Cousy, coach of the Cincinnati Royals, watches his team struggle during a game against the New York Knicks in 1970.

Bob Cousy

named for the inventor of the sport, Dr. James Naismith. The institution has many exhibits to teach the history of the game and has chosen those who have dedicated themselves to the sport of basketball each year since 1959. The Hall of Fame has chosen great players and coaches to include in its exhibits. Getting inducted into the Hall of Fame is considered the greatest individual honor a player can receive. In 1970, Cousy was inducted. Fans of all ages can go to the hall and learn about Cousy and his basketball career. He will always be considered one of the best basketball players in history.

To be inducted into the Hall of Fame, a player must have had a remarkable career. He must also have been a good ambassador of the game. If a player was great on the court but harmed public opinion of the game, he may not be inducted. There have been two famous cases in which great baseball players were not inducted into the National Baseball Hall of Fame. Both Joe Jackson and Pete Rose had careers that qualified them for the Hall of

Bob Cousy *(front left)* poses with a group of former NBA greats who were voted as the All-Time SuperTeam by members of XPRO, an association of retired professional basketball players, in 1996.

Fame, but both were accused of being involved in schemes to bet on baseball. As a result, neither player was ever inducted.

Cousy almost faced the same problem. In the early 1950s, the government exposed a number of college basketball players who had been involved in betting scandals. Cousy's name surfaced as one of those players. A gambler had said that Cousy was involved in betting schemes. Investigators met with Cousy in 1953. They found out that the gambler had been lying. Cousy's name was cleared, and he went on to build a model career.

Conclusion

The name Bob Cousy will be linked forever with the sport of basketball. Bob Cousy has spent his lifetime in the sport, beginning with a brilliant career as a high school and college player, and going on to the professional circuit. After retiring as a Celtics player, he went on to make contributions as a basketball coach and as a television broadcaster for the sport. Cousy also wrote a textbook on basketball, called *Basketball: Concepts and Techniques*. He is remembered as one of the greatest basketball players of all time and one who made an art of the sport on the Boston courts.

Cousy's story goes beyond the world of basketball, though. His life story reminds us of the classic American Dream. His parents came to the United States in search of a better life. When their son was born, they wanted to give

Life After the Celtics

him a better life than they had. They wanted him to grow up to be happy and successful. Through hard work and dedication, they gave him a chance to fulfill his dreams.

Cousy learned from his parents' hard work and sense of responsibility. His countless hours of practice as a young man helped him develop the skills that made him a great athlete. He did not always achieve success quickly, but he never became discouraged. He showed determination, and rose through the ranks at Andrew Jackson High School, at Holy Cross College, and with the Boston Celtics. Along the way, Cousy excited fans and won championships. He also became a legendary Hall of Famer.

glossary

agent A person who helps an athlete negotiate a contract; a business representative.

ambassador An individual who acts as a model representative.

ambidexterous The ability to use both your right and left hands skillfully.

assist A pass made from one player to another that leads directly to a basket.

autobiography A story of a person's life written by that person.

center Usually the tallest player on a team's starting unit; the player most responsible for plays closest to the basket, including rebounding, scoring, and shot blocking.

draft The selection process that determines on which professional teams the top newcomers will play.

Glossary

dynasty   In sports, a team that is seen to dominate a sport by winning most or all of the championship titles over an extended period of time.

fast break   A play that occurs when the offensive team captures a rebound or a loose ball and rushes up the court in an attempt to score before the other team is ready on defense.

forward   One of the two players flanking the center, usually on offense. Forwards play close to the basket, and must be good shooters and rebounders. They are usually taller than guards, but shorter than centers.

Great Depression   A time of poverty in the United States that began in 1929 when the stock market crashed and lasted through the 1930s.

immigrant   A person who leaves one country and settles in another.

junior varsity   A team of younger players who hope to make the varsity team.

MVP   Most Valuable Player, usually awarded at the all-star game and the NBA Finals.

NBA National Basketball Association; founded in 1949. The NBA currently has twenty-nine teams in the United States and Canada.

overtime An extra period played when regulation time ends in a tie.

point guard A guard whose main responsibility is to orchestrate a team's plays and advance the ball up the court.

rebound To retrieve the ball as it comes from the rim or backboard, taking possession of it for either team.

recruit In college sports, an attempt to get a player to go to your school.

regulation time The normal length of time it usually takes to play a basketball game.

rookie A player in his first professional season.

tenement A low-rent, rundown apartment.

varsity A team of the best players in a school.

for more information

ESPN.com
506 Second Avenue
Suite 2100
Seattle, WA 98104

The FleetCenter (Home to the Boston Celtics and
    the Boston Bruins)
One FleetCenter
Suite 200
Boston, MA 02114
Web site: http://www.fleetcenter.com

Naismith Memorial Basketball Hall of Fame
1150 West Columbus Avenue
Springfield, MA 01105
(413) 781-6500
(877) 4HOOPLA (446-6752)
e-mail: info@hoophall.com
Web sites: http://www.hoophall.com
http://www.basketballhalloffame.com

Web Sites

Bob Cousy: The Official Web Site
http://www.cmgww.com/sports/cousy/index.html

ESPN
http://www.espn.com

Find Hoops
http://www.findhoops.com

Hoops Avenue
http://www.hoopsavenue.com

National Basketball Association
http://www.nba.com

Women's National Basketball Association
http://www.wnba.com

for further reading

Bjarkman, Peter C. *The Boston Celtics Encyclopedia*. Champaign, IL: Sports Publishing, Inc., 1999.

Glenn, Mel. *Jump Ball: A Basketball Season in Poems*. New York: Lodestar Books, 1997.

Goodman, Michael E. *Boston Celtics (NBA Today)*. Mankoto, ME: Creative Education, 1987.

Gutman, Bill. *The Kids' World Almanac of Basketball*. Mahwah, NJ: World Almanac Books, 1995.

Hubbard, Jan, ed. *The Official NBA Encyclopedia*. New York: Doubleday, 2000.

Joseph, Paul. *The Boston Celtics (Inside the NBA)*. Minneapolis MS: Abdo & Daughters, 1997.

Myers, Walter Dean. *The Outside Shot*. NY: Bantam Doubleday Dell Books, 1987.

Pietrusza, David. *The Boston Celtics Basketball Team*. Springfield, NJ: Enslow, 2000.

Sullivan, George *The Boston Celtics: Fifty Years—A Championship Tradition*. Bel Mar, CA: Tehabi Books, Inc. 1996.

index

A

Andrew Jackson High School basketball team, 18, 20–21, 22, 27–35, 40, 103
Arkin, Morty, 19–20, 24, 25
Auerbach, Arnold "Red," 59, 72, 86

B

Basketball: Concepts and Techniques, 102
Basketball Is My Life, 10, 22, 30, 77
Boston Celtics, 6, 42, 48, 52–53, 55, 57, 59, 61–62, 64–65, 67, 68–89, 96, 103
  as NBA champions, 77, 79, 82, 83, 86–87
Boston College, 33, 90, 91
Boston Garden, 42, 50, 52, 77, 87
Boston "Tear" Party, 87–88
Brown, Walter, 57–59, 62, 88–89

C

Chamberlain, Wilt, 82, 83, 97

Cincinnati Royals/Kansas City Kings, 91–96
Cousy, Bob
  at Andrew Jackson High School, 6, 18, 22–32, 33, 44, 53, 62, 64, 102
  with Boston Celtics, 6, 62–67, 68–89, 96
  as broadcaster for Celtics, 96, 102
  childhood of, 9–21
  as coach of Boston College, 90–91
  as coach of Cincinnati Royals, 91–96
  in Hall of Fame, 6, 96, 97–100, 103
  at Holy Cross College, 6, 33–34, 39–53, 62, 64, 102
  marriage to Marie "Missy" Ritterbusch, 53–55
  NBA championships won, 6, 77, 79, 82, 83, 86–87, 89
  in NBA draft, 56–61
  as NBA Most Valuable Player, 7, 75, 89

Index

parents of, 5, 9, 10, 11, 18, 28, 34, 38, 39, 102–103
retirement from Celtics, 84, 87–89, 90, 102
summer at Tamarack Lodge, 35–39

D
DiMaggio, Joe, 17

G
Grummond, Lew, 18, 22, 24, 25–27

H
Haggerty, Ken, 33–34, 40
Heinsohn, Tommy, 74, 75
Holy Cross College, 6, 34, 39, 40–52, 53, 103

J
Jones, K. C., 78, 84
Jones, Sam, 78, 97
Julian, Alvin "Doggie," 34, 39, 40, 43, 44–49, 53, 59

K
Kerner, Ben, 59, 60, 62

L
Lapchick, Joe, 43–44
Long Island Press basketball league, 20, 23, 24, 25

M
McCauley, Ed, 68, 69, 72
Minnesota/Los Angeles Lakers, 66, 79, 83, 84, 86
Musicant, Artie, 34, 35

N
Naismith Memorial Basketball Hall of Fame, 6, 97–100
National Basketball Association (NBA), 6, 7, 52, 56, 60, 61, 67, 68, 69, 71, 72, 75, 77, 78, 79, 83, 87, 89, 90, 91, 94, 96
  all-star team, 61, 89
  NBA draft, 56, 60
National Collegiate Athletic Association (NCAA) tournament, 42, 43, 48, 52
National Invitation Tournament (NIT), 52, 91
New York Knicks, 28, 61, 68, 71

O
O'Connell Playground, 12, 19–20, 24

P
Philadelphia Warriors, 82, 83

R
Ritterbusch, Marie "Missy," 53–55
Russell, Bill, 72–73, 74, 75, 78, 97

S
Sharman, Bill, 68–69, 97
Sheary, Lester "Buster," 49, 52
St. Albans, Queens, 11–12, 17, 28, 39
stickball, 10, 12, 14
St. Louis Hawks, 72, 75–77, 78, 82

Syracuse Nationals, 69–71, 72, 78

T
Tamarack Lodge, 35–38
Tri-Cities Blackhawks, 57, 59, 60–61, 62

About the Author
Rob Kirkpatrick is a book editor and freelance writer living in the New York City area. While finishing this book, he enjoyed watching the Duke Blue Devils men's basketball team win their third NCAA championship.

Photo Credits
Cover © Bettmann/Corbis; pp. 4, 36-37, 47, 50, 54, 58, 70, 79, 80-81, 85, 88, 92–93, 95, 98–99 © Bettmann/ Corbis; pp. 8, 16, 41, 65, 73, 76, © AP/Wide World; pp. 13, 23, 29 © courtesy of the Queens Borough Public Library; p. 63 © courtesy of the Basketball Hall of Fame; p. 101 © AP Wide World Photos.

Series Design and Layout
Geri Giordano

www.ingramcontent.com/pod-product-compliance
Lightning Source LLC
Chambersburg PA
CBHW041112070526
44584CB00002B/139